# The Zero Stress Zone

## "A Layman's Guide to Stress Management"

## TOP HARRIS

authorHOUSE®

*AuthorHouse™*
*1663 Liberty Drive, Suite 200*
*Bloomington, IN 47403*
*www.authorhouse.com*
*Phone: 1-800-839-8640*

*First published by AuthorHouse 9/13/2007*

*ISBN: 978-1-4343-3251-6 (sc)*

*Printed in the United States of America*
*Bloomington, Indiana*

*This book is printed on acid-free paper.*

Dedicated to "Deedo," my beautiful baby boy.

Dad loves you… Always.

# *Contents*

# _Prologue_

Webster defines stress (stres) as; 1. Mental or physical tension, strain, or pressure. 2. Strain or straining force.

I had several goals in mind when deciding to create this guide to stress management. First and foremost the objective is to assist people in dealing with day- to- day stress by helping them to identify coping strategies. Developing personal strategies has proven immeasurably helpful throughout the course of my life; consequently I believe it is important to develop individual stress management tools for regular use in our pursuit of a stress free environment. The place I want people to get to? "The Zero Stress Zone."

Realistically, zero stress is a lofty goal that will probably never be realized because life brings with it stressors and outside influences over which we have no control. But, like the quest for perfection, although we may never attain it, the outcome of the effort makes us better persons in the end. In the quest for "stress free," at minimum we can become stress resistant.

Second, I seek to foster an understanding of the relationship between thoughts, emotions, and actions. Controlling the outcome of a situation sometimes becomes easier if we understand that we can; in fact, control the outcome of situations. For instance, as adults, and even during our pubescent years we have experienced jealousy in one form or another. It is in the context of stress management, that we must realize jealousy is a normal emotion. Perhaps we were the jealous boyfriend, or the envious employee, or even the competing sibling.

Whatever the case, although we all feel these emotions, we don't all go on a murderous rampage as a result. Something stops us from acting adversely in response to those powerful feelings. Although we are not always able to control our emotions, we can actively control our responses to those emotions. Controlling action or reaction is the key to self-maintenance of one's own mental health and stress reduction. In the pages that follow we will discuss self-initiated control mechanisms and how to apply them effectively.

The third goal is to demonstrate that it is possible to manage stress without becoming slaves to therapy, drugs, or other medical or scientific remedies. By no means, however, is this book intended to be a substitute for legitimate medical or psychological diagnosis. Commonsense will be the word of the day. Commonsense will form the foundation of the coping strategies that will emerge from the reading. The concepts, in most cases, are so simple you may ask yourself why you had to buy a book to tell you these things. In the end though, if you ask yourself that question you will have gained an understanding of how simple stress management can be.

Lastly, the information will be delivered in layman's terms in order to break from the mind numbing scientific and academic approaches commonly associated with stress management. I am not a Ph. D., nor am I a scientist, philosopher, or intellectual. I am an average person, of average intelligence, drawing from personal experiences and the experiences of others. In fact, many of the concepts to be explored were passed to me from my mother, Ruby, and are referred to throughout the text as "Rubyisms."

Although from a blue-collar background, I understand that stress does not discriminate. It affects white collar, blue collar, and even no collar people. Therefore, within this text, no one; is more important than the other. Having been exposed to the multitude of stresses we all face on a daily basis, I place emphasis on dealing with stress at its most basic level, and thus the average Joe and the CEO are synonymous when it comes to individual stress management.

Ultimately, the overall objective is to provide basic, real world stress management skills in a clear, concise, simple manner. There are no absolutes, and to every rule there are exceptions, so this book is not intended to be the end all, be all, answer to stress. What it is, however, is a guide to better understand those things we can control, thus improving our ability to cope with stress and maintaining our own mental health.

# Chapter One
## Open Your Umbrella

I remember those winter days back in elementary school when the weather turned from sunny perfect to rainy miserable. My mother would get us up early so we could get ready for the day. As we awoke we heard that unmistakable sound of the hard rain pouring against anything standing between the black clouds and the ground. Immediately we wanted to get back in bed to escape the wet misery that awaited us outside. With Miss Ruby, however, that was not to be.

Instantly, anxiety took over because we knew it was going to be cold, wet, and miserable. Imagine leaving the warm comfort of sheltered slumber to enter the unrelenting rain soaked outdoors. On top of that, it wasn't even to go somewhere fun, it was to go to school for Pete's sake. We dreaded everything leading up to that first step out the door and often spent many of our initial waking moments trying to figure out how not to go outside. "My stomach hurts!" "My head hurts!" "My throat hurts!" "Heck, one of these has got to work." It never did.

Then, it was time to leave. We couldn't get a ride because, well shoot; our parents had to walk to school ten miles each way, in the snow, on unpaved roads, with holes in their shoes, and carrying all their books. If it was good enough for them, apparently it had to be good enough for us, given the fact the school was only a few blocks away and we had all the latest clothing advances; oh yes, and lockers where we left those things we did not want to carry.

We braced ourselves for the inevitable. We stood in the doorway and took a deep breath to gather our courage. We agonized over the drenching that was about to occur and we gave one last thought to feigning illness. All options exhausted we pushed open the door and stepped into the nightmare it had taken all morning to construct. But then, we paused, just for a moment. We suddenly remembered that crappy Christmas present we got from Granny. We ran back inside to the closets in our rooms and dug to the bottom of the muck until we found them. There they were; those ugly plastic umbrellas we hated so much.

Back to the front door we went. Up went the umbrellas and out we burst into the day shielded from the release of the clouds. Suddenly, the rain didn't matter. Heck, even having to go to school didn't matter. Before we were half way there we began to have fun. We began to see that this little bit of water wasn't going to hurt us, nor was it going to slow us down. The day went well. We saw our friends, we stayed inside to play games, and essentially, we did the same things that would be done on any other day.

As a child I surely didn't give any thought to the affects the stress and wasted energy had on me. However, today I realize the anxiety I felt on those rainy days was real and; it was self-induced. What I failed to do in my youthful inexperience, was look at the big picture. I didn't consider all the elements involved in all that was going on around me. If I had, I would have realized that those things I was stressing over were going to happen no matter what I did.

Now, by no means am I saying that as children we should be expected to recognize stress and develop strategies to deal with it. I am simply pointing to the simplicity of the childhood situation to illustrate the simplicity of the solution. There is no way to stop the rain. When Mother Nature says it's time to open up the floodgates it's going to pour no matter what we do. The rain here serves as a metaphor for the numerous, and often less than pleasant things in our adult lives that are going to come no matter what. It could apply to paying taxes, going to the dentist, meeting the parents of your fiancé, or even speaking with a police officer who has just stopped you for a traffic violation. In my profession as a police officer I have observed subjects regarding the latter on many occasions.

Some people who come in contact with police under these circumstances create stress for themselves. They attempt to question the validity of the stop, the officer's competence, the law, and even the officer's motives. It is not my intention to offer my opinions regarding people's right to inquire as they see fit, nor is this a dissertation on the legal nuances of a traffic stop. It does, nevertheless, pose the question: Is there anyone who believes that confronting, or challenging an officer with these questions, in the middle of a traffic stop will make things better as far as the outcome of that contact?

I have seen many traffic stops. More often than not, this type of confrontation only serves to piss-off the officer. The outcome is certain to be less favorable for the driver than if he, or she, had simply taken the one violation ticket. Instead, the driver now has a three, or four-violation ticket born from the closer scrutiny the officer suddenly felt compelled to undertake as a result of the driver's inquisition. Let's analyze this situation.

The traffic stop is the rain. It is happening and we can't do a thing to stop it. The inquisition serves as the creator of the driver's anxiety. The result is the unnecessary elevation of our individual stress levels. The answer: Open your umbrella.

You can stay dry in this situation by simply evaluating possible outcomes. Ask yourself this question: What behavior should I exhibit to make this situation as favorable as possible for me? The stop has occurred and brought with it some external stressors. Internally, however, we have the capability to respond to these stressors in such a way that we minimize the bad affects on our mind and body. When people talk to me about their experiences in these situations and they express anger over the officer's actions, I always ask, "Did your actions in this matter make your situation better, or worse? More often than not they look at me with a confused look as if to say, "I never thought of that before."

As is the theme of this book it is a very simple concept. You have to actively control your urge to exert yourself in situations where the control, authority, or power doesn't belong to you. No one likes to get tickets; but in the event you have to get one, why not get the one that has the least negative impact on you?

In all aspects of our lives we can open our umbrellas to shield ourselves from the rain that is sure to come. In family situations, work situations, and any other situations that arise, the constant is that there will be components present, over which we have absolutely no control. The key is to think our way through to the most favorable end possible. This does not require higher education, extensive training, or a century mark IQ. A graphic example of the concept was illustrated in a work situation I observed in my work-place.

It was a very busy night as a result of a driver's license checkpoint that was being conducted. Numerous cars were impounded as a result of unlicensed and uninsured drivers. The process started with the completion of tow forms requiring extensive vehicle and driver information. The vehicles were then towed to a storage yard where they would stay until the driver's either acquired a license, or brought in a licensed driver to the station to get a vehicle release authorization. That authorization costs a pretty penny and is a time consuming process, as is the process of entering the vehicle, driver, and release information into the computer. That job belongs to the records clerks. On this night there was only one clerk working due to a number of sick call-ins. Needless to say she was bombarded with impounds and releases, and to complicate matters the irate owners were all standing at the front counter impatiently waiting.

The volume of work clearly rattled the clerk and the mob outside simply added to her pressure. On numerous occasions she made grunting noises and pulled at her hair in a visible display of stress. It built up over a few hours until she simply stopped working and put her head in her hands as if to say, "I can't take it." She was worked up to say the least. Fortunately her sudden stoppage coincided with the arrival of the overlap clerk who was preparing herself for her shift at the desk next to clerk number one. In a matter of minutes clerk number two was logged on and ready to go.

She began to handle the continued onslaught of drivers and impound forms while clerk number one took her long anticipated lunch break. While she was gone I watched the other clerk perform the exact same functions as the first. Time and time again she would bang away at her computer keys then get up to help the next owner and so on. In contrast to the first clerk, number two maintained a constant smile and pleasant demeanor. Never once did she get rattled by the obviously angry mob outside, or by the volume of work. Within a short time she was in a constant rhythm and the whole process was flowing smoothly. Number two got more done in the hour that number one was gone than number one did in the hours prior.

Curious about how she was able to maintain such a stress free appearance I asked her for her secret. She looked at me, smiled and said, "I let those outside know that I can't go any faster, but I can go a whole lot slower." As she turned to walk away she looked back with a devilish grin and said, "They seem to get the picture." I looked over at the hoard of drivers and noticed there was, indeed, a calm over them that was not previously there.

Suddenly it dawned on me what had happened. Number two simply opened her umbrella and dealt with the rain. It was clear that she could only do what she could do. She embraced that fact and simply turned to do the job at hand, knowing that the checkpoint would result in this amount of work. She also knew that checkpoints like these are necessary and are apart of her job. Essentially, she accepted the inevitability of the day's work knowing it had to be done in order for her to get paid. She shielded herself from the bad elements and, to use the analogy from my childhood, she stepped out the front door, opened her umbrella, and went off to school. When I asked her if she was stressed by the task at hand she replied, "It has to be done, what else can I do? I can either do it or be unemployed. To me the choice is clear."

Clerk number two had mastered the art of opening her umbrella as a means of minimizing the stressful situation she had to encounter. She altered her mindset so that the outcome, again, was most favorable to her. Clerk number one did not control that which she could control, so that which she couldn't control, controlled her.

Speaking of control here is *Rubyism* number one*: "I run this and you run around in it!"* This one is a classic that served as a constant reminder that I was not in charge. I had to do what I was told or face the painful consequences; painful being the operative word and huge understatement. You see, my mother was quick with the switch. She would frequently go to the nearest tree, grab a good-looking limb and pull it off. She would then pluck the leaves from it as she walked toward me, creating a psychological impact, to go along with the physical one. Once the switch was naked the pain would rain down on my behind something fierce.

It quickly became clear that I brought these storms upon myself. It was very simple; do what I was told, follow the rules, and I avoided pain. What's more? I began to avoid the stress of placing myself in positions that might result in Ruby's wrath. Doing the right thing became second nature and it was born from a choice. Either do it; or feel it then do it. Either way it was going to get done. I opted to zero my stress and go with the option that was most beneficial to me. It was also much less painful.

Knowing when to open your umbrella is the key. In real world situations we are faced with this Rubyism frequently. At work, in the classroom, in sports, you name it. The technique I developed to deal with these situations in my life is basic pain avoidance: a "do that which causes the least amount of pain" approach. Apply this concept to situations in your own life and consciously decide to avoid pain. Every time you are confronted with a situation that makes you feel tense, uncertain, or just down right angry; embrace that emotion. Accept that you feel the way you do. Then ask yourself, "What do I do now?" Often when I take the time to actually ask myself this question, I have slowed down my reaction process and allowed for discretionary time to formulate the most favorable response. I call this technique, Enhancing Your Calm.

Enhancing your calm is a means by which to lessen the negative impact of the stressful situation by taking the time and effort to recognize your possible responses and how those responses are going to affect you in the end. Imagine that your boss gives you an assignment that you don't necessarily like. Suddenly you are faced with a number of choices. You can tell her that you don't want to do the task, in which case the outcome is negative for you and the stress will increase. You can question the task, in which case the outcome is negative for you and the stress will increase. You can display a negative attitude and complete the task, in which case the outcome is negative for you and the stress increases. Or, you can simply say "ok" and complete the task, in which case the outcome is positive for you and you zero your stress.

Your first three options have the increased potential to cause pain, or at the very least discomfort. The pain symbolizes those potential negative repercussions that may result. You could receive less than favorable evaluations or reviews, disciplinary action, termination, and the most serious in my opinion, negative recommendations for future employment opportunities. Why cause yourself the aggravation associated with these foul outcomes? Why not take the final option and maintain your positive reputation? In the event you don't want to stay at this job and your plan is to seek employment elsewhere, at minimum, you leave armed with positive recommendations.

In the end you will have opened your umbrella and shielded yourself from those things you can't control and you will have taken control over any stress that those things bring. You have choices. Your handling of the situations that will confront you is a conscious endeavor. You have the power to think your way through them to the best outcome possible.

With me it took a little practice, but ultimately, I became proficient in opening my umbrella. So proficient in fact, instead of waiting for the rain, I often open it in anticipation, gaining a head start on stress. In essence, I have transformed my thinking to be prepared and often, have thought my way through issues before they happen. This kind of preparation is a kin to ensuring you always have your umbrella with you and available for use. Have it. Use it. Maintain it. You will feel the difference.

# *Notes*

## _Chapter Two_
## Get in the Shade

Summer was in full swing and the hot Nevada sun was beaming down on us something terrible. I was sitting in the boat having a beer while my friends were doing likewise. Some were in the water, while others were relaxing on the beach. The lake and all the anticipated festivities of spring break promised a weekend of splishin', splashin', drinkin', and just plain funnin'. I would soon find out that things would not go as planned.

We had been on the water since early in the day and as we moved into the afternoon we felt the temperature rise steadily. We made efforts to beat the heat. We jumped in the water, we drank ice-cold brew, we rubbed ice on our bodies, and we went out on the boat to seek refuge in the artificial breeze that heavy throttle created. In spite of the heat, all in all, it had the makings of a very fun outing.

As we neared the end of the day we packed it up, secured the boat, and headed back to our hotel. Drained from equal parts of intense heat and intense alcohol consumption, I decided I would forego the evening activities and stay in my room to recoup. I must say, it was probably the best night of sleep I had in a long time.

The next morning it hit me. My skin felt like it was on fire. I had no idea what the problem was, and I got really scared. You see, I had never before experienced sunburn. As luck would have it, or more accurately, as my stupidity would dictate, I got the mother of all sunburns. My friends, the veteran outdoor guys, told me what it was, and aside from the winces of pain, my reaction was that they were out of their minds. I have seen people with sunburn and it never looked like it hurt this much. There's no way this is sunburn. Ultimately they convinced me and I began my recovery therapy with mega doses of Aloe Vera.

At the time the pain consumed me and I didn't think about much else. I would later come to understand the meaning of my ordeal; an ordeal that was all the more shocking to me because I am a black man, and up until this time I was so naïve that I thought black folks couldn't get sunburn. Believe me, I am no longer that naïve. In retrospect, it is clear that I had not had an understanding of the sun and its power. I would later find out that along with the heat came other more dangerous elements like UV rays, etc. These elements were immune to the water, ice, cool breezes, and even ice-cold beer. You're shocked right?

Eventually this experience was behind me, but my love for water recreation was growing. In time, through the expert guidance of my friends, the weekend warriors, and my painful ordeal, I learned that I had overlooked the one preventative measure that would have saved me from the evil intentions of that hot summer sun. It's so simple, I kick myself in the butt every time I think about it and I tell myself, "Next time; get in the shade Dummy!"

Sometimes we go out into the sun because we want to. Other times we go because we are put there by circumstance. Whichever the case, we need to remember to make use of available shade. Sit under a canopy, cover bare skin, find a tree, do something to make use of the shade for periodic respite from not only the oppressive heat, but the other unseen elements as well.

The sun in this story represents those oppressive elements that are present in our lives. Those hard to put up with, and hard to escape issues, or people that weigh heavily on the mind and spirit. Think about what those things may be in your life; an overbearing boss, the deadline sensitive job, the less than understanding teacher, or maybe the pressure of numerous issues that are all present at once. Unlike the umbrella strategy, under these and other like circumstances, the umbrella may not be enough to beat the heat. In these instances we are confronted with more than just the simple discomfort discussed in the previous chapter. We are actually facing active stressors, which, if left unchecked, have more serious repercussions. The heat is on.

*Rubyism: "that lady doesn't need anything from you, but you do need something from her. You need the grade so go to class, shut up, and pass."* Wow! This one rings in my ears as if she just said it again. I think of this lesson frequently because situations have continually surfaced since the high school event that spawned it. In college, in the service, at work, and even in happenstance occurrences this lesson is very effective. Allow me to explain.

It was a school day not unlike any other. I went to school and attended classes, socialized, and all the other things teenagers do on any given school day. Unfortunately, the only bad thing going on at that time was also present as it had been every day for most of the semester. I was still in Mrs. Simmison's Algebra class. I'll be very blunt with you; I hated her. In my mind she was responsible for every ounce of grief I experienced in high school.

Mrs. Simmison was a very demanding teacher. Very demanding! She had very little personality and, in my opinion, she was basically just a very angry person. Now, I had other demanding teachers and challenging courses, however, this algebra class represented my academic nemesis. I simply dreaded going to this class. I would get worked up two periods prior and it would often last until the end of the day. The end result was that I could never pass her class and I failed it two semesters in a row. I begged for a transfer to another class. I pleaded with my mother to make them put me in another class, but as was her M.O., I had no hope of that happening. She has always been a "you need to face your problems" type of parent. Ultimately, there was no escape.

One day my mother became furious about my continuous failures and she sat me down to begin the inquisition. We had been there before and each time I went right back to the same failure prone behavior. This time, however, was different. It looked different. It sounded different. It certainly felt different. In a manner I can only describe as eerie, she began to speak through me. I could actually feel it.

She asked me why I was having these problems and my answer was a little different than it had been before. I had always simply answered her with a half hearted, " I know Mom I'll do better." All the while believing that next semester I would get a new teacher and my problems would be solved. This time I put my feelings out there and I was adamant in my delivery. "I hate her and she hates me! She will never pass me because she is the devil and that's just the way it is!" At the time I didn't realize how close I was to getting slapped. Boy am I glad Mom chose a different approach.

She looked at me and said, "Son, that lady is gonna go home and eat her dinner. She is gonna go on her vacations. She's gonna get her paycheck and she's gonna enjoy her own life. She's gonna get her next class and she is gonna go about her business everyday with or without you. She isn't gonna think twice about you. *That lady doesn't need anything from you, but you do need something from her. You need the grade so go to class, shut up, and pass."* Mom's delivery compelled me to rethink my approach. Part of it was because I knew she was right, but mostly it was because she scared me.

I went back for the new semester with a different attitude. Armed with Ruby's ammo I did exactly what she told me to. I went to class every day and kept my mouth shut and my opinions to myself. Even when I wasn't paying attention I made it look like I was paying attention. I made the teacher feel as if I were a changed person, and although I really hadn't changed much, the façade was powerful nonetheless.

Although Mrs. Simmison's attitude toward me was consistent, and as witchlike as ever, eventually I experienced a change in my own attitude. I quickly learned that this was a much better way of doing things because I didn't have to carry the stress with me when I left the class. As shocked as I was at this changing dynamic resulting from this new found stress-free mode, you can imagine my surprise when, at the end of the semester I received a passing grade in the class. Whew!

The lesson I learned was that by consciously controlling those things I have control over, which in this case was my own behavior, I eliminated the day-to-day stress, as well as that associated with bringing another failing grade home to Miss Ruby. Ultimately it even led to a better knowledge of math and an even greater knowledge of people and the application of people skills.

While I was in the middle of this crisis it was clear to me that the heat was brought on by the teacher. What I would later find out, however, is by getting into the shade I was able to prevent any additional adverse heat related problems. Moreover, I realized that heat is a fact of life, especially when it comes to human relations. We will find heat in many situations we face throughout or daily lives. The key element is gaining an understanding of how to protect ourselves from the stress generated in these situations whether it is truly brought on by external forces, or as in my case, is more internally generated.

Everybody has a Mrs. Simmison somewhere in his or her life; that person or that thing that keeps the temperature up and the shade to a minimum. I submit that in these cases we have a lot of control. Primarily our control is over our own behavior, and ultimately that behavioral management leads to control over stress and its negative influences.

Having served in the Unite States Marine Corps I have seen first hand how mindsets and internal mechanics can be altered in a very short period of time. Marine Corps Boot Camp is one of the most powerful examples of this positive, medicine free, behavioral modification. In a little over three months a person can go from whatever they were before enlisting, to a disciplined, polished, and well behaved individual. Aside from the obvious tenacity and controlled craziness bred into

Marines in order to carry out their tough mission, they are also taught to be polite, respectful, and are thoroughly entrenched in honor and esprit de corp.

Basically, recruits are retooled through a program designed to strip away those traits that are not desired of a Marine and they are rebuilt to Corps specifications. The significance of this process is that it takes place over a relative short period of time but the effects are life long. We would be hard pressed to find anyone who would disagree that in this environment there is a significant amount of heat. Taking this into account, my contention is that even in situations of intense heat it is possible to alter behavior to the positive.

In the Corps there are drill instructors that facilitate the change. They reprogram the recruit's thinking until he or she is on track and performing in a manner consistent with the desired standards. In our personal lives we can be our own drill instructors, retooling and rewiring ourselves to cope with the lesser intense heat associated with most daily endeavors.

I utilize a technique I call Self-talk. In this process I go over in my mind issues I might face in the future, then formulate responses and make adjustments. This is done during a time when I am not facing the heat so that when the heat comes I will be prepared. Let's call it mental sun block. If used regularly it performs much the same as the gooey applicant we put on our skin, in that it gives us protection from the get-go. Instead of reacting to the pain caused by exposure we are proactively preventing the exposure all together. In even more simple terms we are thinking our way through the heat to an outcome that is desirable to us.

Pose this to yourself: When it is hot outside do you get in the car and turn on the heater or the air conditioner? If you said the heater then you may have issues this book doesn't address. But, if like everyone else you answered air conditioner, the simplicity of the concept is already clear to you. We can beat the heat and lower our stress by turning on our stress conditioner. If we cool our environment we make our surroundings more comfortable. In comfort we can better think and work our way through what ever we are facing at any given time.

Half the battle is recognition of heat sources. If you know where it is hot you can plan avoidance or coping strategies accordingly. The key is to plan. If you consciously tell yourself you are not going to get burned you will do the necessary things to protect yourself. Make it a point to maintain your comfort level and above all else, do not become your own stress factory. Often times we manufacture stress in situations where the external factors are not all that big a deal. Some of us run our stress factories at full bore creating self-generated heat and stress related mental and physical problems that often lead to medical issues. Why?

We have the ability to control our own heat, thus, we can significantly reduce the ill effects and increase our stress-conditioning threshold. Like any machine when our body works for prolonged periods of time, or it is exposed to stressful situations it has the tendency to heat up. To combat this, periodic breaks from the heat are often enough to keep stress in check. I have found that taking a break from whatever I'm doing, and listening to music, tends to decompress me. After a short break, I'm ready to get back at it until I need to return to my musical break room for additional decompression.

Some of us fail to make use of coping strategies and subscribe to the thought that we have to meet heat with heat. It's kind of like getting in that car on a hot summer day and turning on the heater. It doesn't make a whole lot of sense. We feel if someone yells at us we have to yell back. If someone confronts us we become equally confrontational. Most of the time the original problem or issue never gets resolved because the focus becomes the confrontation. Similarly, we raise the heat level in situations that are basically so stupid that they often defy reason. I experienced one such incident while driving with a friend of mine on the highway near my home.

Daniel has been my friend for what seems like thousands of years. I know him as if he were me. This made it all the more shocking on this day when he unnecessarily lost control and created stress not only for himself but for me as well. While we were driving down the highway in the fast lane another car drove up behind us and got really close to the bumper. It was clear that the driver wanted to pass us in a big way.

It was equally clear from the flashing of his head lights and the honking of his horn that he wanted us to move out of his way and he had no intention of going around us. Given this scenario, here is your first stress reduction test. Take a little time and think it through. *What should Daniel have done?*

If you said move over and let the car proceed, then you passed. What Daniel did, however, was slow down and began tapping on the brakes as if to say back off! The driver from the other car became enraged and continued to follow very closely only now he was using highway sign language to express his anger. Mind you, we were still traveling at fairly high speeds on a highway occupied by other motorists also traveling at high speeds.

This was a dangerous game Daniel was playing to say the least. Suddenly the guy tried to move to the next lane to pass but Daniel moved over to cut him off. The driver moved the other way to attempt a pass but met with the same result. I noticed that Daniel was extremely agitated and displayed the same angrily contorted face of the guy behind us. Very quickly I became confused about who was doing what to whom.

Both these irate drivers continued to play this game to the exclusion of all else. It continued for a couple of miles even though I was yelling at Daniel to knock it off. He was so angry though, that he actually couldn't hear me. I was, in effect, tuned out as was any regard for safety. Fortunately slowing traffic up ahead forced the game to slow a bit and the driver passed us flipping us the bird as he went by challenging us to stop the car so he could, in his words, "kick our asses." He got in front of us and began to return the favor by stopping abruptly and not allowing us to pass. This went on for about a mile before a passing police officer brought the game to a halt and the driver drove off out of sight.

The lesson here is that there was a whole lot of stress going on, not to mention the potential for injury or death. Let's look at the possible consequences. We could have crashed and killed ourselves; killed some innocent motorist, or we could have been dealing with a person with a gun and a desire to use it. None of these options are favorable. For purposes of this book let's focus on the stress issue.

The key point that I later tried to explain to Daniel and I want to express here is that it's clear the driver behind us was a jerk. As Miss Ruby would say, "he is a jerk today, he was a jerk yesterday, and he'll be a jerk tomorrow." So, why let him push your buttons to the point you invite unnecessary stress upon yourself. In this incident I swear Daniel probably aged five years with the amount of stress he heaped on himself. If Daniel had simply moved out of the way and let the jerk pass at the beginning of this mess, the stress of this situation would have passed right along with him. Think about it; this incident was over what? A piece of highway that doesn't belong to any of us anyway. I later asked Daniel why he didn't just let the guy pass. He explained that if the guy hadn't been such a jerk he would have. His answer confused me because there was no logic to it. What was there to win? What was there to gain by putting people at risk over that stretch of highway with some guy you will never see again? This one is a no-brainer. Just move out of the way and get in the shade.

This incident provided a contemporary example of the need for simple and effective stress reduction strategies. If Daniel had thought through this before hand, perhaps he would have already solved the problem before it actually became a problem. More importantly he would have reduced his stress and my anxiety over the safety issue, had he just kept it simple and avoided the discomfort.

As a result of this incident I began to think of how I have behaved on the highway in the past. It was not always the most favorable for sure. Consequently I now, routinely enhance my calm whenever I am faced with similar circumstances while I am driving. I do not allow people to penetrate my stress bubble. If you want to pass me that bad, be my guest. I consciously tell myself not to give a second thought to would be jerks on the road, so consequently I don't. The benefit is that I arrive at my destination without the heavy baggage stress brings with it. Ultimately, I'm stress free and cool because I always find the shade.

# *Notes*

# Chapter Three

## Identify the Fault Lines & Relocate

Have you ever had that conversation? You know, the one in which you talk about where you would most like to live based on the type of natural disaster that takes place there. It probably sounded something like this:

> *"I would like to live in the South because they only have storms or maybe a hurricane every now and then. Hurricanes aren't that bad because you have plenty of warning before they hit." "Well I would like to live in the Mid West because they only have tornadoes but the serious ones don't occur that often and besides everyone's got a storm cellar to hide in when they hit." "Me, I would like to live in the North East. It gets cold and there are snow storms and even blizzards but at least it's expected, and there are weather forecasts to tell when it is going to hit. "*

It sounds funny but we rationalize things in just this way. The one thing that never seems to reach a comparative level of rationalization, however, is the natural disaster commonly associated with the West. You guessed it; earthquakes.

Being a California native I have lived through earthquakes and the threat of earthquakes all my life and I can tell you when one hits, it's no fun. The problem with earthquakes is that they come on so suddenly, that there is absolutely no warning. The ground just seems to erupt at your feet, shaking violently. In those more intense shakers, buildings come down, pipes break, and fires break out. It's harrowing to say the least.

The difference between earthquakes and those natural disasters commonly associated with other parts of the country is that the others offer some level of warning that minimizes the "caught off guard" effect. In some cases residents have enough time to prepare for the problem so as to protect their property and their person. With earthquakes, however, that just simply is not the case and it is the quickness with which it comes on that causes most of the fear, anxiety, and stress. Within the context of this book, earthquakes, or "Stress-quakes," as they will be referred to throughout this chapter, symbolize those incidents of stress that come on suddenly and without warning.

Now, even though we cannot yet effectively predict earthquakes, science has identified where they are most likely to occur. Through years of research it was discovered that fault lines in the earth's crust are the centers of activity. Fault lines are areas where the plates of different sections of the planet come together and it is here that underground shifting and realignment takes place. Consequently, since we know where they occur, the only way to really avoid becoming a victim is to know where the fault lines are and relocate. Since we can't predict them with certainty, we should simply avoid them altogether. In real life it's easier said than done because in most cases relocating may not be feasible. Still there are two choices: relocate, or deal with it.

Case in point: Denise, a mother of five, obviously has her hands full given her number of offspring. The many responsibilities that come from raising one child are multiplied as are all the related stressors. Can you imagine? In this setting there are enough external stressors that she doesn't need to create more, however, in a recent incident she manufactured stress unnecessarily; that is to say it was preventable.

On this day it was busier than most because of school related matters and such. Denise was on the go the entire day. Toward the evening she needed to go to the local shopping mall for some items and she let her children know of her plans. Her 14-year-old, third of five, wanted to go, so Denise took her along.

When they arrived at the mall, Denise went right for the items she needed and she began to scoop them up. During her shopping spree her tagalong said she was going to go look at some clothes in another store and she would return shortly. Once Denise was done with her purchases she went looking for her daughter and quickly found her in a popular youth clothing store.

Immediately the girl started begging for mom to buy her something. Mom had neither the money, nor the inclination to buy her daughter anything at the time. The daughter, however, was adamant about her need for this specific item and became, quite simply, a pain in the butt. Denise stuck to her guns and refused to give in to the tantrum; consequently, her daughter began to pout, and huff and puff in a continuing tantrum like fashion.

You might be thinking that maybe this runs deeper than just this day, or there are some parenting issues here that led to this in the first place. Such is not the case, however, because I know this family intimately and Denise is a very strong parent and her daughter usually a well-behaved teen. In this case it seemed like just an isolated eruption, sort of like that which kids experience from time to time.

This incident caused Denise to undergo severe stress as I would later find out when she called me to decompress. She was extremely angry and obviously way above her stress norms. It wasn't the tantrum that was the big deal. It was the fact that the tantrum came on the heels of all the day brought with it to this point. It was simply the straw that broke the camels back.

When I spoke to her during her decompression she was beside herself. She was ranting and raving about how her daughter got on her nerves and really pissed her off because she'd had so much more to do and now she was off track. How many times have we seen this, or even done it ourselves; exploded at something small that became huge simply because of where it occurred during the day.

In this case I listened to Denise as she told me that she knew her daughter would start asking for things once they got to the mall. She said it always happens, not to the point of a tantrum, but it happens nonetheless. The gist of Denise's issue, as she exclaimed was, "I knew she was going to do that. I should have just left her at home!" I let her exclamation sink in for effect before I shot back to her; "Why didn't you just leave her home then?" Silence was the response.

Denise knew she had been busy all day and she knew she had much more to do yet. Because she had this knowledge she should have known where she was as far as her stress norms. Thus, it can also be said that if she were paying attention, she would have seen the fault lines that were clearly visible. In its simplest form Denise knew exactly where the fault line was because she knew that her daughter would do what she did. In fact it was a common occurrence. Given the predictable nature of the behavior why, then, didn't Denise just avoid the stress-quake? She had the ability to relocate away from the fault lines by leaving the daughter at home and avoiding the inevitable rumbling.

In earlier chapters, we discussed pain avoidance and you don't have to be a missile mechanic to grasp the concept that here, we are talking about very visible external indicators of future stress. Recognition of these indicators is the key to proactive stress reduction through fault line avoidance. Equally important in this regard is our recognition of our internal stress norms. Where are our lines and what are our limits?

Once we understand our stress norms, or tendencies we can begin to actively control them. Take, for example, banking. I hate banking. I hate that long line that curves through the center of the bank. I hate watching five employees walking around doing nothing while two tellers are trying to help the hordes of people. I hate that there is never enough parking outside banks, and that there are never enough deposit envelopes at the automatic teller machines. For me, banks bring stress.

When I began to understand myself and my stress I recognized that I needed to control these influences in order to maintain my mental health. Consequently, I took advantage of a relocation strategy by doing all my banking online. I have direct deposit, direct bill pay, and I use debit cards whenever possible, virtually never needing to carry cash. How does this help me? Well I can bank from the privacy of my own home and eliminate all the stress that comes from a visit to the bank.

This is not an extremely stressful situation but as we saw from the previous example, things add up so I have developed strategies to keep things from piling up. The simple strategy of recognizing my fault lines, i.e.; the bank, and relocating, i.e.; online banking, has helped me avoid preventable stress, and has significantly reduced the build- up helping to maintain my stress norms. Maintenance of stress norms is important and as in Chapter Two I will use another traffic example to illustrate this point.

In the context of relocation it is not always about the physical. Sometimes mental relocation is equally powerful in removing us from the fault lines. How many times have we been in our cars on the highway in bumper-to-bumper traffic, when we look over at a car next to us and the driver is bobbing his head. Maybe he's snapping his fingers, playing an invisible drum set, or just plain rocking out. Whatever the case we conclude he's either a mime gone nuts or, he's listening to some music that moves him. I'm sure the latter is usually the case. The key point is that, if we take time to notice, he's usually smiling or displaying an attitude much different than the other drivers around us.

Most of the others appear angry, impatient, and just plain tired. On any trip of even short distance we see numerous nonverbal exchanges between people who are simply fed up with the traffic, each other, and the discomfort associated with long periods in seated positions. When on the road, in traffic, I have studied this dynamic and asked myself why most people seem to be adversely affected by the stress of highway traffic, and others seem to not be affected at all. The answer came clear when I combined my observations with my own response in these situations.

I am a music lover and I have a CD collection of all my favorites. When I'm at home listening to the songs, especially those that have specific meaning to me, I become one with the music. I get in the same mode as that driver I spoke of earlier. Click! It suddenly dawned on me. The music takes me to another place; a place that feels good. Remember we made fun of those people on the road because it looked like they were in a different place, well guess what? They were. They had merely relocated mentally and placed themselves in a position where the stress from the external forces was not adversely impacting them. Do they like traffic? Not likely. But it's clear they like where the music takes them.

Those of us who are daily commuters know we have to sit in traffic and we know it's frustrating. We also know it's a part of our daily life that is not likely to change any time soon. These are the fault lines that we know are present and that we have the power to avoid, even if we can't avoid them; so to speak. The music can take us to that other place where we are stress free. It allows us to cope with this inevitable situation bringing it to the most favorable conclusion for us. Getting lost in the music is a simple way of relocating until we reach our destination.

Miss Ruby had her own way of dealing with stress, and the Rubyism for this chapter was born from the stress brought on by her two sons constantly buzzing in her ear. We would ask question after question even after we had been given more than sufficient answers, or we would constantly ask for things that we had no chance in hell of ever getting. "*I tuned you out*" was her reply in these situations. She even had an invisible radio knob turning movement she did with her hand to let us know she just changed the station, and in affect, tuned us out. It really meant go away you're bothering me and was usually the precursor to the swift backhand she was famous for. We learned quickly.

What she had really done, was create a mechanism by which she was able to mentally relocate and avoid the stress we brought on. By tuning us out she not only sent the message that she didn't want to be bothered, but she kept herself from succumbing to the adverse impact of bratty little kids who were, more often than not, pains in the butt. This is not to say she wasn't a great mother because she was. So much so I can't even describe it, but there were times when she needed a break. Since she couldn't permanently physically relocate, she simply mentally relocated. The only part I'm not sure about is whether she relocated herself from us, or us from her. That one still has me wondering.

Another technique I have used is reflective relocation. In layman's terms this means thinking of things that remove me from this stress filled environment. When we are stuck in traffic it is a perfect time for reflection. Turn it into your time and reflect on the things that occurred that day, or the things that are still to come. Make use of the time that you have to spend in traffic anyway, by thinking of pleasant things such as loved ones, friends, or happy occurrences, etc. This works well whether or not you're in music mode. I consciously reflect on these things giving rise to good feelings that override the bad feelings associated with the stress of the highway moment. And although we have made extensive use of the traffic example in this book, these concepts can be used in any situation where you find yourself facing recurring stress generators, or fault lines.

Of course trance like immersion should be avoided in the name of traffic safety. For those who think these particular techniques raise driving safety issues; don't employ them. A premium should be placed on safe vehicle operation and if you cannot walk and chew gum at the same time, ere on the side of safety. It would, after all, be extremely stressful to crash while you're de-stressing.

# _Notes_

# *Chapter Four*

## Weather the Storm

Twas the week before Christmas and all through the mall, all the creatures were stirring; shopping and all. This included me and Mom, who were out getting presents to complete our lists and who, like everyone else were moving from store to store in the Christmas shopping frenzy. It should be noted that I was about 32 years old at the time and I was six feet two inches tall weighing about 235 pounds. Though my age and size have no bearing on the shopping experience, it will become painfully significant as you read on.

The mall was built like most; a long isle flanked by numerous stores from one end to the other. We were walking side by side amongst the hoards of people minding our business, people watching and such, when I noticed an item in a store that caught my attention. As I rubbernecked to get a better look I felt the sudden pain of an impact to the back of my head. The force slammed my head forward and knocked me off balance a bit as the blow wasn't even remotely expected. I turned around expecting to engage someone who would obviously have to be my size or better to even attempt such an attack. What I found, as I whirled around poised to strike back, shocked and frightened me. The shock? The culprit was my mom. That's right, it was Miss Ruby. The fear? Someone as small as she is, and at her age, still packed such a wallop.

In this crowded place with all eyes watching, drawn by the pop sound made by her slap to the back of my bald melon, I stood, wondering what the heck her problem was. I was angry and embarrassed and I was quite sure there were finger marks on the back of my head. Finally, in stunned disbelief I asked her why she hit me. She replied with the Rubyism, "I just wanted to let you know I still can!" I looked at her for a moment as she looked right through me and I put my head down and said simply, "yes Ma'am." We went on with our shopping and the event was put behind us; behind us but not forgotten, especially by me.

I remember the feeling I had that day. It was like I wanted to retaliate but I knew it was futile. If you recall, I spoke of Miss Ruby's discipline in previous chapters so you know retaliation, or even disrespect was out of the question. Okay, I was scared, but it wasn't like I could do anything about it anyway. She was mom and she could do what she did and that was that. There was however, a lesson learned that day that I carry with me and now share with you. Under circumstances in which you are powerless to make change, sometimes you just have to weather the storm. Sometimes you have to grin and bear it.

Weathering the storm is a strategy unto itself, containing remarkable stress reducing qualities. These qualities may not be readily apparent unless you know what to look for. You might think that based on the previous chapters, the only way to become stress resistant is to avoid situational stress altogether. In most cases those strategies work well and are very sound. We cannot however, leave out of the discussion those instances where they may not be applicable.

In those situations where we are unable to open our umbrellas, get in the shade, or relocate, we must still practice stress relief if we are to achieve maximum stress resistance. If we know that stress is coming, or that it may be ongoing, we can prepare ourselves mentally to weather the storm. Let's face it; sometimes we just have to endure the stress either out of necessity, or in some cases as part of a "means to an end."

In my job there are certain rules in place that dictate the road to promotion. Each Chief has brought with him a standard set of promotional requirements outside the commonly accepted hard work and dedication. Under the current boss, education is the primary element in his success formula. It was, therefore, in my best interest to get back into college and complete both a Bachelor's and a Master's degree. This caused a major problem for me because I hated school. I really hated it.

Ultimately, I did complete my educational requirements, however, during the entire six-year process, I felt the constant stress of school and school related work, especially in the Master's program because so much is expected of a student at that level. When I combine these rigors with my fulltime job, and the raising of my family, it is clear that there was constant stress and there never seemed to be a let up in the storm. In that regard, I quickly formed the opinion that I was simply going to have to ride it out. There was no way around it, over it, or under it. I had to go through it and I had to continue to march even when I wanted to just give up. The end result of my efforts was rapid promotion, continued possibilities for advancement, and an enhanced capability to provide for my family.

The thing that got me through it all was that I realized what the mission was. I kept my eye on the prize and I simply willed the stress to another place where it could not hurt me. Because I knew it was there and that it was going to be there for a long while, I was ahead of the game because I was able to front-load my preparedness instead of reacting to whatever arose. In other words, I knew it was there, I prepared for the long haul, and I knew it was the means to my desired end. I call this technique re-directed focus. Redirecting focus simply involves taking the focus, or emphasis off that which causes the stress and placing it on the good that will come at the end of the process.

If we begin with the end in mind it is possible to reduce the stressors of any situation so they do not overwhelm us, even though we know there will be a storm. If we aggressively attack a problem keeping the end, or desired end in mind we can render the negative stress we may incur along the way, ineffective. For a case in point let's revisit Denise.

Denise is a very nice person who is the one that all of her many friends want to be around all the time. When they go out they want her there. When they stay in they want her there. When they party hearty they want her there; and when they go into relax mode they want her there. As Miss Ruby would say about Denise, "When she goes to the gathering every one wants to sit at her table." It's definitely true in this case.

With this popularity comes some strife because even on those occasions when Denise just wants to be alone, or to stay at home with her kids, the onslaught of calls continues and everyone is trying to get to her table. The problem is, Denise is very social and adores her friends, but she often likes to sit in bed and watch T.V. or knock around with her kids. The dilemma you ask? Well, she makes up stories to tell her friends as to why she doesn't want to go out, or have them over.

On one such occasion I was at her house visiting, when her phone rang. Based on her response when she answered it, it was clearly a friend on the other end. I could only hear this end of the conversation but it was clear the caller wanted Denise to go out later that night. Denise agreed and the plan was set. Strange though; as soon as she hung up she looked at me with a disgusted face and said, "I don't want to go out tonight. I just want to stay at home," and she frowned as she went back to what she was doing before the phone call. I was dazed and confused, as I tried to make sense out of what I just saw. I had to ask, "Why didn't you just tell them you didn't want to go?"

Denise broke into a long dissertation about how her friends don't understand, and that she feels like it's rude to just tell them. She even offered that she didn't want to deal with the stress of making her friends mad. The gist of her answer was that she felt it was better to have something come up later that would allow her to cancel on the date without hard feelings from the caller. Again, I had to ask, "Why didn't you just tell them that you didn't want to go?" This time she sat in silence with a thought provoked look on her face. I was sure she was now thinking more deeply about my question.

The bottom line is that Denise created more stress in lying to her friends and having to carry it with her all day until she dreamed up an excuse, than she would have if she had simply said in the beginning, " I don't want to go because…" Through the discussion that followed Denise related that she had always lied to her friends when she didn't want to disappoint them. She felt it was too much of a load to bear to have them mad because she told them the truth, so she lied. Makes sense to me. Not!

I asked Denise to examine her own feelings and to be honest in her assessment of this situation. My intention was that if it worked for her I was just going to leave it alone. I didn't have to because after giving it some serious thought, she looked at me and said, "It would probably be easier if I just told the truth in the beginning because they're going to be mad at me either way." She continued with, "Better that they're mad at me up front and over the truth, than after a whole stressful day over a lie." I concurred.

The simplicity of it is Denise would have saved herself hours of stress by just riding out the brief storm that may have resulted from being up front with the caller. I said may, because it is conceivable the up front approach might have been appreciated by the caller and others, and that no storm would have resulted. Either way Denise lowers her stress levels by embracing the drama initially, instead of creating additional, more intricate drama over the long term. Simple isn't it? I knew you would agree.

We should also examine the dynamic that occurs in a person that would get mad at someone for being honest and up front. How would you react if you were the caller in this scenario and your friend told you straight out that she did not want to go out that night for whatever the reason? Would you be angry? Would you have a negative reaction? Or would you simply take it for what it is? Sometimes people just don't feel like going out, or they feel like doing something else. What's wrong with that? If you were full, having just eaten, would you eat again because you were afraid to tell the person inviting you that you already ate? If you have issues in this regard then you do have issues. Stress issues.

How would you feel if you were the caller who later found out your friend lied to you and never had any intention of going out that night? You would probably be peeved to say the least. It may even cause a prolonged angry episode that has long lasting effects on the relationship. These negative effects create the kind of stress that is totally avoidable by all parties by simply weathering the storm and being upfront with each other.

I said earlier that sometimes there is no alternative to riding out the storm and you've seen examples of the simplicity of the concept. It should also be noted that within the confines of a "ride out the storm" type incident, there may be opportunities to utilize the previous strategies for portions of the problem. That is to say, that even in situations where we have no control over the stressful event, we can still control the effects of the stress on us by employing any of the previous strategies, weathering the storm, or a combination of these, depending on suitability.

Weathering the storm also has one other positive attribute when used effectively. It helps to build stress tolerance. The more we use it the better we feel about it, especially given positive outcomes. I submit to you, however, that in cases where the event may lead to a negative outcome, you are still capable of willing a positive effect on your mind and body by developing the skill to ride it out. In the end the event itself will be over and you will be on your way to the next evolution. What you will carry forward is either a load of stress, or an empty stress container. Which do you think will be the lighter load?

# <u>*Notes*</u>

# *Chapter Five*

## Increase Your Stores for the Winter

Nature provides several examples of how increasing on-hand supply of food, or other necessities significantly increases the chance of survival in the wild. Bears gorge themselves with fatty foods prior to hibernation to build up stores of fat within their bodies. They do this so that while they are inactive and unable to hunt for the winter, their bodies can draw from these fat stores to ensure survival. Come Spring they will emerge, a bit thinner for ware, but alive and ready to hunt. Similarly, squirrels gather hordes of nuts and store them in their winter homes so they can draw from their naturally produced pantry until Spring arrives and they can go shopping again. Even we stock up on food and water when times are lean to ensure we have enough to get through to more fruitful times. This survival strategy has maintained life for thousands of years and forms the basis for another stress survival technique I call "increasing stores for the winter."

Winter in this analogy represents those lean times we know are going to come like clock work. They could be tax season, seasonal job layoffs, trips to the dentist, expensive holidays, returning to school, etc. In my experience these events and others like them have the tendency to produce large amounts of stress. This is especially true if you may owe on your taxes, or if you're about to experience the seasonal job layoff. It's true if you hate the dentist as most do, or if you have a large family all expecting gifts during the holiday season, or even if you are going back to school for a new experience under new circumstances.

The stores in this analogy represent stock- piles of stress reducers in anticipation of the recurring events. Our fat stores and nut pantry are represented by the preparation we put into dealing with known future events. Let's take taxes as our first example.

Every year at the same time we have to file our income taxes with both our state and federal governments, except in those states with no state income tax, but always in the case of the feds. It occurs like clockwork with the dates and deadlines known by everyone. Why then, do we procrastinate on completing and submitting our tax forms? So much so in fact, the post offices stay open until midnight on the last day to accommodate all the last minute filings. We heap hordes of stress upon ourselves during these times worrying about making the postmark cutoff, or filing for an extension, or even making that last minute appointment with our tax preparer. Why?

Let's also look at those who know, or reasonably should know they will owe on their taxes. Often these folks wait until the last minute to deal with how they will pay what they owe. Will I use my hard earned cash? Will I deplete my savings? Will I take out a loan? Or will I pay in high interest installments? Stress; stress; and more stress.

The way to combat these issues and to provide the best outcome for you is to prepare ahead of time for this inevitability. Eliminate the stress by dealing with this problem before it becomes a problem. You can project what you will owe and begin to set aside the necessary funding you will need. You can force yourself to complete your taxes on the first available day instead of the last. You can have in place a plan to deal with the sureness of your dilemma. It's mostly mental, in that all you have to do is gear your mind to prepare for the winter. If you knew that a severe snowstorm was approaching and that you were going to be confined to your house until it passed, would you wait until the storm arrived to check your empty cupboards for food and then kick yourself in the butt? Probably not. It's more likely that you would go out prior to, and stock up on food, water, batteries, etc., so you could ride out the storm.

It seems simple because it is simple. Mental preparedness and action planning reduce or eliminate stress when used pre-event. Let me reiterate; it is mental. We have to consciously make these efforts and in doing so we can effectively deal with issues when the pressure to get it done is at its least.

Another way to build up those winter rations is to make use of the tolerance you build up during the small storms, so that when the big ones hit, you are already ahead of the game. If you develop sound stress management skills regarding the little things, your momentum will be such that you can keep it rolling even in more severe stress situations.

As a worker bee, I had a supervisor who was a micro manager above all else. His supervisory style required him to have his thumb on his subordinates so they knew he was in charge. He knew it all, had seen it all, and had done it all. Do you know anybody like this? Well, it was uncomfortable to say the least, but I had a choice; make it work for me, or against me. I chose the former.

I knew that everyday I was going to have to work under these conditions and I knew that I was never going to change this individual's style. I decided therefore, to make it work for me. I challenged myself to come up with coping strategies to deal with this situation. One of them was to choose this person as my formal mentor via my agency's career development plan. The benefit to me was that instead of having a confrontational relationship with this guy, he was now forced to take on the nurturing role of my mentor and coach. Let's face it, I had forgotten more about my job than he would ever know, but the bottom line was, he was in charge. I used this strategy to solidify a relationship that was more conducive to my own well-being and although his personality was still screwy I now had built up the means by which to have it affect me less.

This supervisor had ten to twelve others to supervise but I knew that I would have to deal with him on a recurring basis throughout the shift. Because he could not devote all of his attention to me and I had now altered the relationship to the positive, I was simply building up my stress tolerance, and as you will see, it would later come in very handy.

Fast-forward three years. I was now the supervisor responsible for the same group of ten to twelve individuals. I had a manager who I answered to and guess what; it was the same guy who supervised me as a line troop, only now he could really devote a lot of attention to me because I was the only supervisor he had. This turn represents the increasing severity of the storm, in that now I did not have the luxury of having the dictator's attention divided between several other people. It was just me.

Luckily, or by design, depending on your point of view, I had built up my stress management stores and I was fully capable of using them to effectively reduce the potential negative impact of our manager, subordinate relationship. Because I had done it for so long in smaller, recurring instances, it was much easier to deal with on this grander scale. In the end this manager left the department under less than honorable circumstances, and I? Well I'm still here; and virtually stress free.

Storing up supplies is essentially about two things; getting ready for the then, now; and establishing a foundation of tolerance to draw upon in future, stress producing incidents. In both cases the fundamental element is prior mental preparation. Prepare for the inevitable so that even when the outcome is bad, it's not nearly as overwhelming as it would have been without the prep.

I told you earlier of Miss Ruby's tendency to go to the rod for discipline when I was growing up. To her credit, she applied that discipline fairly in that it hurt the same every time, and she did not discriminate. My brother got his hide tanned on more than a few occasions as well. It is the contrast between our responses to the whoopings that provides the next example of the "increasing the stores" concept.

I provided Mom with many valid reasons to let loose on me because, quite frankly, I had a tendency to be more than rambunctious. Okay, sometimes I was just down right bad. In any event, I knew I was going to get it. I didn't always know when or where but I knew it was coming. What I learned very quickly was that the punishment was inevitable given my tendencies toward certain behavior. My brother was much the same; not quite as often, but very similar. There was however, one telling difference between us. When it came time to get our just deserts, I would stand there and take it. My brother? Well, he would take off running.

At first I thought he had the right idea. You know that sort of, "know where the fault lines are and relocate" kind of right idea. In this case though, we had it all wrong. Even if we ran, we had to come back eventually, and therein lay the problem. Although I immediately got whatever pain was coming to me, when it was done, it was done. My brother on the other hand, would run away and forego the immediate pain, only to have to deal with the stress of knowing he was going to get it when he eventually got home. In fact, it was going to be a whole lot worse than I got because now Miss Ruby was truly pissed.

Imagine the psychological impact of knowing you have to go back to the place where tremendous pain awaits and the only choice you have is, when you're going to accept your fate. The stress this generates can be overwhelming, but preventable as well. While my brother was out contemplating the severity of his predicament, I was done with mine and was now in the healing process.

The lesson here is my brother failed to realize that building up his stores would eliminate the additional stress, even if it didn't eliminate the pain. If he had done as I did, and accepted the hardship up front, he would have removed any additional stress and been able to more quickly move on to the next episode, which in this case would be things returning to normal.

# <u>*Notes*</u>

# *Chapter Six*

## You Can't Stop the Wind, So Adjust Your Sails

What do you do when your electricity has been turned off because you didn't pay the bill and you can't get it turned back on right away? You light a candle. What do you do at a restaurant when you only have enough for dinner, or dessert? Make a choice: sweet-tooth, or hunger pains. What about when your car breaks down and you won't have the money to fix it until payday? Take the bus. Although the alternatives in these examples are not the most enviable, they are most applicable in the reduction of stress.

Sometimes we have to realize that we may not be able to change external goings on, thus the only way to reach the desired end, is to make internal adjustments. Take for example being out on a sailboat. The sails are up and the wind has you cruising along the water enjoying the breeze and the summer sun. All is good; until, suddenly the wind picks up and you begin to lose the control you enjoyed moments ago. You are at the mercy of the air stream that is propelling the boat toward open seas. The moment of truth is quickly upon you. Either drift at the wind's whim, or take charge of your situation and make the necessary corrections.

An experienced sailor would quickly begin to adjust the tack by reversing the boom in order to use the wind to change the boat's course and maneuver the craft back toward homeport. Understanding that the wind cannot be stopped, the adverse impact of the situation can be avoided by simply adjusting the sails. Small alterations to the position of the sails are often enough to turn the craft around and put it on the desired course.

Fine-tuning our responses to stressful situations is as easy as adjusting the sails. What we must do, as the experienced sailor does, is learn to control it: to manipulate it so that we are not negatively impacted. The key is the recognition of unchangeable conditions. This is vital because it is the lack of recognition that creates the stress that is so damaging to our mind and body.

In the workplace there are some people who complain about everything. You've seen them, those who are never happy, constantly expressing their unhappiness through thought and deed. The worst culprits create stress for others by constantly provoking, antagonizing, and instigating. What these people have failed to do is to recognize two things. First, they do not understand their own stress threshold and they are in fact creating enormous stress for themselves. Second, they fail to realize the issues they face are often unchangeable, thus, the stress they are creating is truly unnecessary.

Now, it can be said that sometimes we just want to cause a ruckus to vent, or to create change, or even to simply get the satisfaction of expressing ourselves while making our points. It is, however, when we fail to distinguish between intentional action, and that which is uncontrolled, involuntary action, that we have a problem. If people create stress for themselves, or others, every time they are involved in a situation, it is probably their response techniques that are failing them. This is especially true in those cases where the situation itself is unchangeable.

I was at the Los Angeles International Airport not too long ago preparing for a business trip. It was mid-day and as you might imagine it was very busy as the airport was jam packed with people arriving and departing. One of the busiest and most crowded areas was the security checkpoint leading to the gate area. People and their luggage were everywhere and all were being funneled through what I can only characterize as more of a choke point than a checkpoint. All the people were being squeezed into single file lines so they could go through the two metal detectors and their belongings through the X-ray machines.

Before I continue, I must provide the time frame of this trip in order to provide perspective. It was shortly after the attacks on the World Trade Center on 9/11. This is significant because any knucklehead should have known that following this horrific event things were going to change at airports. Nowhere were the changes more evident than at this outer security checkpoint.

As I waited my turn in the shuffle toward the metal detector, I noticed some commotion to my right at the second of the two detectors. A man, probably in his early fifties, was engaged in an argument with the security personnel at that station. Out of sheer nosiness I suppose, I moved closer so I could hear what was going on. What the heck, since I had to be in that slow moving herd, I figured I might as well take advantage of the impromptu entertainment.

The man was very upset because security personnel asked him to remove his shoes so they could be checked. This should not have been a surprise to anyone because everyone was being asked to remove their shoes to ensure contraband would not walk through security and onto an airplane. The security personnel were extremely professional in the way they handled this situation, but they were equally adamant that either the man's shoes were checked, or he did not fly. The man came unglued and completely lost control. He questioned them over and over again as to why they had to search his shoes. He repeated several times that he knew his rights and that a search warrant was needed to go through his shoes in this way. He asked for and spoke with the supervisor who told him the same thing; take off the shoes, or just take off.

After several minutes, one of the security screeners pulled the man from the line and over to a special security area out of my earshot. Based on the demeanor of the ranking security person, I can only assume that the facts of life were being explained to the man in no uncertain terms. Finally, the man gathered his belongings, wandered over to the security stations, removed his shoes, and after a detailed security examination was allowed through to the gate area. Of course, now, not only had the man caused himself significant delay, he caused delay for everyone else as well.

Eventually, I got through security and over to my gate. Wouldn't you know it? There he was; the angry man from the checkpoint; and he was still angry. So angry in fact, he was red about the face and his bottom lip quivered. He was beside himself, talking to anyone who would listen about his ordeal. No one listened for long as they seemed genuinely disinterested in the man's issues. He was basically talking to himself.

I took inventory of what I was seeing and what I had seen at the security area. I formed the opinion that this man was going to implode. He looked as if he were about to blow a gasket. He was so stressed, that every visible muscle was rigid and he was sweating profusely. He remained discolored and visibly on edge until I lost sight of him once we boarded our flight. I'm sure by the attention he got from the flight attendants, he was still causing a ruckus during the remainder of the five-hour flight.

I asked myself what it was I had just witnessed. The answer I came up with was this guy failed to realize the unchangeable nature of the issue he was faced with at the checkpoint. He was obviously unable, or unwilling to make the necessary adjustments to ensure the most favorable outcome for him.

The fact is, security has become very tight at airports and understandably so. Plenty of warning is given to potential flyers as to the intensity of the security process and the need to arrive early.

What then, was this guy's malfunction? Well, he failed to adjust his sails and continued to battle an unchangeable situation. The odd thing is that he had nothing to hide. He did not have contraband, nor did he pose any other security risk. What he did pose, however, was a stress risk. He single handedly stressed himself to the point of near stroke, and he stressed everyone else who was delayed and/or irritated by the man's tirade. Guess what? In the end he still had to take off his shoes.

What I learned from this episode, as Miss Ruby would say frequently, "Some things are what they are." It means some things can't be changed, therefore, why try? Make the adjustment so that you come out on the longer end of the stick. Decrease your stress by recognizing there is no need to stress over this thing because it's not going to change anyway. Spend the energy finding a way to make it work for you, instead of against you. I'm certain that there wasn't anyone who went to the airport wanting to take off their shoes. In spite of that, the likely stress-reducing response of the other people at the checkpoint was, "take off the shoes. It's quick, painless, and I like the security of knowing everything is being checked." Do you see the adjustment?

If this man had an issue with his treatment, a better tact would have been to go with the program then file a complaint on the back end. Even if the complaint went nowhere he will have been heard, only this way he would not have had to undergo all the damage he did to himself on the front end. Remember, if he wanted to fly out of this airport, he was going to have to take his shoes off no matter what. I suppose the alternative would have been to adjust his sails to the point that he refused, at which point I guess he could have driven to Cleveland.

It's funny. People like the man in this story, get mad if there is too much security, then they get mad if something happens when there is not enough security. It's a very perplexing concept. What is clear, however, is that people like this are constantly stressing themselves under whichever circumstances are present. These individuals are failing to recognize and accept responsibility for their own stress management. It takes a little effort to gain an understanding of self, but that effort is dwarfed by the energy it takes to be like the airport guy. Take the time to recognize the circumstances around you. Develop your nautical skills and don't fight the wind. Adjust your sails.

# *<u>Notes</u>*

# *Chapter Seven*

## It's a Mirage

Is that water on the horizon? Let's get closer and take a look. Looks like water, but it seems so far away. Let's keep going we have to get to it eventually. Man, we've been chasing this ocean for a long time yet it seems just as far away as when we saw it the first time. I give up, it's too far away. I give up.

Funny how those mirages work. Desert heat and sand, fooling you into believing there is water out there when there is really only more sand and dryness. These beliefs can be equated to the feeling we get when we believe that our issues are over, or that which stresses us is gone. We see the water and it seems that our prayers have been answered. Unfortunately, like the desert mirage, it is simply an illusion that brings with it added stress.

Imagine how a person in the mirage sequence might feel after thirsting for water under the hardship of desert conditions, then finding what is believed to be water, only to end up with a mouth full of sand. Imagine the dejection, the exuberance, and finally, the realization. The realization is you are right back where you started. You are right back in the thick of helplessness and despair. This is one of the most apropos parallels of real life stress causation, and, as by now should be understood, thoroughbred gray matter is not required to understand the connection.

In our daily goings on, we are faced with so many issues that it can sometimes be a mind-boggling experience just to get through the day. Work issues, family issues, friend issues, legal issues, and just plain old issue issues, confront us causing daily exposure to external stressors. Utilizing some of the strategies contained in this book, we have learned that there are ways to reduce the impact of stress. What we now need to add to the toolbox is the ability to recognize when we have really gotten there vs. thinking we have gotten there.

When I got divorced I went through all of the emotions consistent with an occurrence of this magnitude. I cried, I got angry, I was hurt, confused; heck, I was just plain unhappy. When I started to get a grasp on my feelings, though, I began to deal with the business end of the end, so to speak; the money, property, and other similar issues that had to be taken care of. Initially it created a lot of stress and I had to employ all of my stress reduction strategies to get through it.

The problem arose when everything was decided; she was getting that, I was getting this, and so on. I assumed the whole legal ordeal would be over quickly because we agreed on everything ahead of time. Such was not to be the case. Because we had our names on everything as co owners including mortgages, loans, bills, etc., we could not just simply be divorced. We had to apply for separate lines of credit, we had to sell our interests to one another on paper, we had to go through all sorts of red tape and because of associated costs, we were negatively impacted in our wallets.

Now, after getting myself together regarding the divorce itself, I began to feel good about the things that were going on; not the fact that it was ending, but the way in which I was handling my own mental health. Since it had to end, I saw the end as the area of peace. The area, that once I arrived, would decompress me because the initial emotional upheaval would be in the past. I actually felt relief at the time we finally got it all together and had the agreements in place. In fact, both my ex and I employed effective stress reduction tactics throughout the initial stages of the process and it appeared we had arrived at the Zero Stress Zone. Boy was I mistaken.

Having gotten to where I felt good, I made the error of thinking I was done with stress regarding this episode. Oh no! Now came the judge and all the business issues that I had not considered. I went from enhanced calm to turmoil in a short period of time. Suddenly I was back in stress mode. I think it hit me twice as hard as the initial stress because I was so convinced I was done with it. It was like being on a boat in a hurricane. The storm tosses the boat around like a cork in a bathtub until it reaches the middle, or the eye of the storm. It is so calm and serene, that when you get there you erroneously believe you are through it, only to find out the second half of the storm is yet to come.

The remedy for the mirage? Do not expect to find water where you know, or should know, it's not likely to be. In other words, the external stressors are always there. They lessen at times, they worsen at times, but you can always expect them to be there. It is the absence of external stress that is the mirage. If we use the prior planning model to think our way through situations we will be able to recognize the mirage for it is. As in the desert if we bring water with us, then the mirage we see is meaningless.

Expectation is the key. If we anticipate and prepare for all the possible outcomes, we will not prematurely celebrate and get caught by the backside of the storm. In a work environment I have seen examples of this in the form of employees believing that a change in supervisors is going to remedy all their problems, only to find that the replacement takes on similar or more sinister characteristics than the original. When this happens the stress is magnified because, one; the expectations were high, and two; the disappointment is higher.

What this proves is that we must constantly prepare for issues if we are to maintain stress reduction. Some might say it sounds like it's just as stressful to battle stress as it is to deal with the original stressor. I disagree. If we are prepared, we have already won the battle and the level of stress is automatically lowered by virtue of that preparedness. In layman's terms, if you see it coming, you can deal with it.

Those who live check-to-check as I do, see this all of the time. We pay our bills and feel good for a while because we are seemingly caught up. The stress is lifted and we feel free. It is short lived, however, because some new expense always pops up. In the case of no new expenses there are still the recurring ones. Because it never ends, we have two choices on how we deal with this. We can either stress ourselves every time a bill is due, whether it's new or recurring, or we can recognize that we will always have bills due and just deal with it. It's very simple.

Miss Ruby used to start off some of her lessons with, *"Johnny, Jeffery, Randy...Boy,"* because she would get so mad at me she would forget my name. Finally, it was just, *"Boy, let me tell you something. It's never over. You kids cause me more grief now than you did when you were little!"* I didn't realize it then, but now that I'm a parent of teenagers, believe me it's true. I remember one time I told her I couldn't wait for my boys to turn eighteen and she fell out laughing. I searched for the humor but I couldn't find it. She did though, and then she explained it to me in one laugh encased statement. "Don't hold your freakin' breath."

Miss Ruby provided a great example of the mirage concept when she constantly asked my brother and me when we would be leaving the house to sprout our own wings. I don't remember what our answers were, but I remember that we never really left. In fact my brother lives there still. I left for the military at seventeen and moved out a short time later. I did, however, go home a couple of times when things got rough. Later I would, leave again, but then I would be back until out; stuck. My brother did the same. He moved out for a while but then he was back. Mom would always get her hopes up to have an empty nest. To date it has not yet come to fruition.

The point is that with all the stress we caused her as children and teenagers the thing she held onto was that we would leave soon and take with us the stress we created. Please don't misunderstand me, my mother's intentions were to have us learn to be self sufficient and to survive on our own. She always put us first and we are here today because of her dedication. She still had hopes, as does anyone who is honest with themselves, of being free. And that's where the real stress began.

When we came back, we didn't come alone. We brought girlfriends, wives, babies, and babies Mamas. We brought not only our stress but we multiplied it times the number of heads we brought with us. I am not a mathematician, but if my calculations are even close to correct, that's a hell of a lot a stress. Picture it. Mom raised us until we were able to venture out on our own, she was clear to live her second life and do her own thing, only to have us come back with more baggage than we left with.

In retrospect it wasn't fair to her and though I didn't see it then I certainly see it now. The lesson I learned is that the short lived nature of some things like the empty nest, need to be kept in perspective. In this case Miss Ruby believed that she was done so she geared herself for what should have been the best time of her life. Suddenly she was right back where she started so you can imagine the stress born from the disappointment. She never balked at it though, she took us in every time and she dealt with whatever stress came with us.

In the mirage we must keep things in perspective. Things are not always what they seem and we need to be prepared mentally for the disappointment. One of the strategies I use is to enjoy what little of something there is to the fullest, recognizing that as with life itself, nothing lasts forever. In doing this I eliminate the stress of disappointment because there is no disappointment. I am happier to have had what little there might have been, than I am disappointed by what is no longer. I force the balance in my favor by remembering that sometimes, it is what it is, just deal with it. I'm not sure by who, but I heard it said once, "Don't cry because it's over. Smile because it happened." That's deep.

In a real life application the mirage concept can apply to many things. Buying a car that turns out to be lemon, getting the dream job that turns out to be a chore, finding a friend that turns out to be snake, or finding the love of your life only to discover they are really just sand, happens regularly in the lives of people. Because this is a component of life we need to train ourselves to deal with it so the affect on us is as favorable as possible.

Life is full of great experiences and my life is no exception. If, however, we think life will be without disappointment we are setting ourselves up for the stress that accompanies a lack of preparation. This is not to say we need to approach every endeavor as if it was going to turn bad. We should expect the very best because that's what makes life worth living and that's what dreams are made of. The gist is we need to develop that part of our being that allows us to deal with the issues when they arise, especially when we think there are no issues and in fact there turns out to be.

I have a friend we call Junior, who in July of 1996, was murdered. He was shot by a street thug, as he carried a tray of Bar B Q to his car following a friendly outing. No motive was ever discovered and no suspect ever brought to justice. You can imagine the stress this incident caused Junior's family and friends. With this background let me explain how the mirage effect wreaked havoc on the minds and bodies of those who loved him.

After being shot, Junior went down but did not appear to be seriously injured. People who were there said he was lucid and talking as they awaited the ambulance. Even in the ambulance he was more concerned about the medics cutting his shirt than he was about anything else. He kept telling them not to cut it, he would take it off. Anyone who knows Junior knows he loved his clothes. Finally he got to the hospital and went in for surgery. Again, he was talking all the way there so surgery really seemed like just a formality. He was so upbeat that everyone thought in a couple of hours we would just go see him in his room, no big deal. It was a big deal, however, because the bullet tore his aorta and he bled to death on the operating table. There was too much damage to repair though the doctors gave all they had.

Imagine the stress you might feel over seeing a friend get shot. It's devastating to say the least. Now imagine the relief you feel when you see him looking as if there is no real problem and talking as if he merely stubbed his toe. That relief makes us feel great: right up until the doctor comes out and says he's gone.

After this incident people were in shock. It was strange though, because they were so concerned about the fact that Junior was talking as if everything was ok, they began to concentrate on that element to the point they lost sight of what had really happened. The stress of Junior's death was magnified by the pointing of fingers and the placing of blame. People blamed the paramedics for driving too slow, they blamed the hospital for waiting to long to get him to surgery, they even blamed the doctors as if they intentionally let Junior die.

This was the mirage effect in its purest form. The fact that Junior appeared to be ok lulled everyone into a state of relief; kind of like that water on the desert horizon. The fact is Junior was dead from the initial shot he just didn't know it yet, and of course neither did anyone else.

Ultimately this incident was extremely stressful for all those involved, but it provided loads of unnecessary stress when we began to evaluate the mirage. When we started believing everything about the aftermath was wrong because he seemed alright initially, the effects of the mirage took hold. Something sinister must be going on. How else can we explain it? For months it could not be put to rest because so much effort was being given to finding someone to blame for there being no water. What we failed to do was deal with what was real. Our friend was gone and we now had to heal and move on. The healing process was delayed for a long time because we placed ourselves under avoidable stress. It was avoidable in the sense that Junior was gone and there was nothing that could be done about it. Everything else was just a mirage.

As with any of the other strategies we have the power to control our responses to the mirage. We can condition ourselves to understand they will occur and that we can handle them accordingly. It's as simple as knowing that if you go into the desert unprepared you will experience illusions, therefore, go forth into the desert, but go prepared. Take water with you and ensure you have an escape, or rescue contingency in case things do not go as planned. In other words, bring the stress tools that allow you to see things for what they are instead of what we would like them to be.

# _Notes_

# *Chapter Eight*
## Enjoy the Calm

You might say it is optimism that best describes my approach to stress relief, and to a certain extent you would be right. It's deeper though, than optimism vs. pessimism. It's more about the utilization of common sense and self control. The ability to think our way through things is commonly referred to as, that which separates us from the animals. It's that same thing that makes dogs pee anywhere while we look for an appropriate place. Although we too have the capacity to urinate in public we don't because we think our way through it. We analyze distances, rest stops, restroom facilities etc., and in the event we do choose to go in public, it is a choice.

We can choose not to let things bother us. We can choose what our reactions and responses will be. We can choose to prepare ourselves to deal with stress, or we can choose not to. Ultimately the choice to be stress free is not without work. It takes effort to learn the strategies and to maintain awareness of our stress levels and our coping mechanisms as they apply to one another.

Common sense is the word of the day. Use it to ensure you have the best outcome for yourself in any given situation. If you get mad at your boss you can choose to go off. You may even get the satisfaction of getting your digs in. That satisfaction is worthless, however, unless you can find a way for it to put food on the table. The ultimate satisfaction belongs to the boss because you're looking for a job while he still has his.

Simply put, stress and anger management make us feel better in the long run. The outcomes are better and we begin to enjoy the calm that it brings. The calmness becomes the norm so eventually it becomes easier and easier to control the impact of stressors.

I have been told on many occasions that it seems that nothing bothers me. I take that as the highest compliment but quite the contrary is true. I am bothered by many things. The difference is I don't let those things consume me to the point I am not in control. I maintain control of my actions, reactions, responses, and outcomes so I don't have to feel anything but calm and the results are always favorable to me.

I would like to provide one last example to drive this point home. When I was in middle school and on into high school I was not part of the good looking crowd. In fact I considered myself ugly by comparison to most of my friends. They were the devastatingly handsome bunch that always got the attention of girls wherever we went. They always hooked up while I often became the fifth wheel so to speak.

In the beginning it bothered me tremendously, you know, "why can't I be like them?" Eventually, however, I began to notice that those relationships never lasted and that the pretty boys, although they met a lot of people, never really had anyone. Often I would ask the girls why they ended the relationships and the answer was commonly, "he was pretty, but that was all there was." I began to recognize what I was coveting wasn't the answer. The answer was within me.

I found that my friendship with these same girls was lasting. I was always invited to the parties and my parties were always packed as well. These same girls would begin to like me as the time we knew each other went on. What it revealed to me was that I had something to offer. It wasn't great looks, but it did look great. It was personality. I had to hone that skill because I was never the guy that had the girls go "goo-goo" as soon as I walked in. I had to get to know them; and them me.

As a result I have no complaints about that time and it really prepared me to utilize the same tools in my adult life. Today I am much the same as then, only now I fully understand that things are what they are and I am what I am. I enjoy the calm that understanding brings me. I chose not to stress over my shortcomings and I chose to develop my strengths. I could have chosen to stress myself over it and the result might mean that I would never be secure in my own skin. Perhaps I might try to be something I'm not, or worse,

I would not have developed the personality I feel has kept me in this stress free place.

Enjoy the calm that comes from being stress free. Make it happen. You can by using the simple strategies we have discussed. Remember common sense and self control form the foundation. The rest is built on making choices that have the best possible outcome for you. When you get there you will know it, and when you arrive my welcome is extended to the Zero Stress Zone.

# *<u>Notes</u>*

# *Epilogue*
## Black Clouds

On October 4th, 2005, my eighteen year-old son Dennis was murdered by a coward who had nothing in his heart but hate, hell-bent on hurting someone just for the fun of it. My son happened to be in the wrong place at the wrong time and was lost to us entirely too soon. Given my intense love for my boy, I was, and continue to be, devastated beyond belief. No parent should ever have to bury a child; so you can imagine the grief and emotions such an event causes.

My offerings in this book were completed prior to the passing of my son; consequently, I had them to refer to during this, my darkest hour. Although my grief is often unbearable, and given my profession my disdain for the perpetrator extreme, I made a conscious effort to practice what I have preached. I must say, difficult does not adequately describe the application of these concepts under these circumstances. I have never been faced with this type of crippling emotional despair and the associated stress at any time in my life; therefore, I initially questioned my own commitment to the concepts.

Ultimately I am beginning to implement my own strategies and make decisions that will get me where I need to be regarding a positive outcome. As a result I am seeking grief counseling with a professional and hope to reap much from those encounters. I have surrounded myself with friends and family, and I am receiving unsolicited support from countless others to round out the external support components that are vital during a time like this.

In this case, the recognition and use of the support components are directly related to the stress reducing strategies I have discussed. I sat down and mapped out a framework that I believe will be most beneficial to me. I am also utilizing each of the concepts at times when the wave of grief rolls in and the external support is gone for the day. As I write this, I am being struck by that wave, but because I have chosen to relocate through this writing, I feel stronger and more capable of handling it. Remember the control is yours.

Ecclesiastes Chapter 3, Verses 1-8 says that there is a time for everything under Heaven, and whether you are religious or not, under conditions like the one I am going through, there is a time for grief, crying, and withdrawal. At some point, however, we must gain control so that the time for healing and stress reduction can take place. Although it may seem self serving, these concepts are working to get me through, and I hope we all can benefit from the power that comes from being stress free, stress resistant, or simply stress aware. The Zero Stress Zone has become a powerful place for me. I hope it is for you as well.

Made in the USA
San Bernardino, CA
06 April 2017